BLUE, THE BLOODHOUND THERAPY DOG

Enjoy Blue's book
Jan Evans Knight
Blue
&
Redford-in
Training

Copyright © 2014 Jan Evans Knight
All rights reserved.

ISBN: 149492529X
ISBN 13: 9781494925291

My friend, Jon, wanted a bloodhound,

He liked its behaviors and looks.

Bloodhounds are large, have long ears and nose,

Like you see in some movies and books.

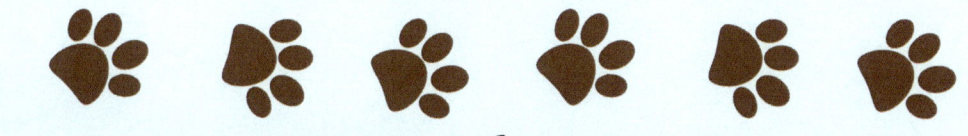

Jon searched and finally got Blue,

He was happy to have a new pet.

And when Blue was a very young pup,

He was fun and Jon didn't fret.

But Blue grew and became quite active

And Jon began to worry.

Blue became quick, noisy, and naughty,

Something had to be done in a hurry.

Blue would break out of his crate,
Chew Jon's socks and shoe laces,
Then dash around his house
As if running in races.

Blue liked to howl and escape,
He liked to mess up Jon's bed.
"He was getting too big to tackle,"
Jon sadly said.

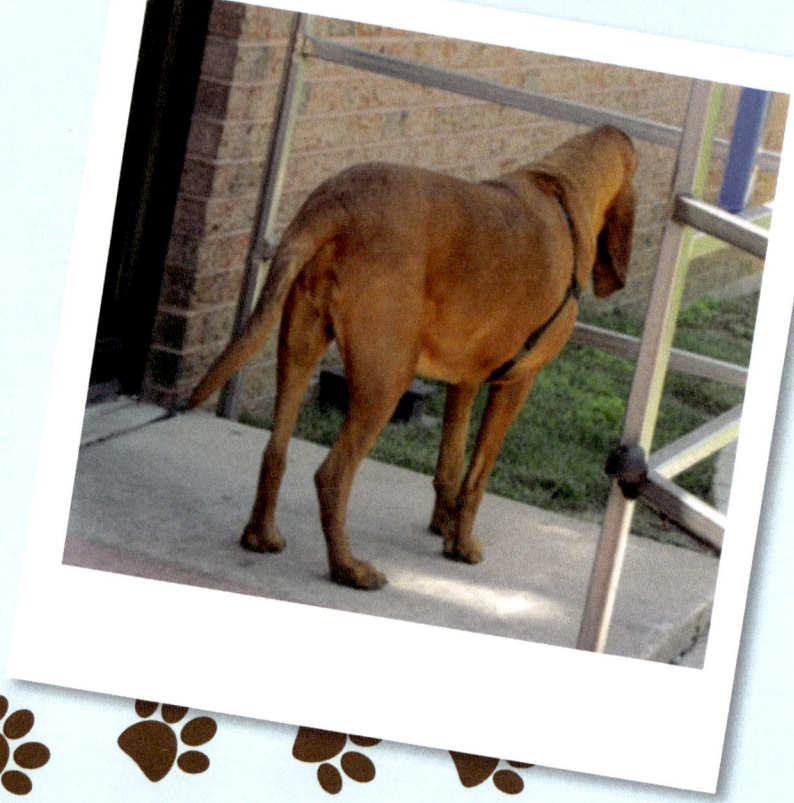

Blue would knock down Jon's fence

And run down the street.

While Jon ran behind yelling,

"Come back! Want a treat?"

So Blue came to my house

One January day,

Because Jon sadly decided

To give him away.

As a ten-month old puppy,

Blue moved in with me.

He weighed eighty-one pounds,

Tall and red as can be.

The first thing Blue did,
He paced in the yard,
Checking the fence,
"Would an escape be hard?"
But the fence was strong,
Blue didn't want to flee.
He has food, space, and love
Blue's thrilled living with me.

Blue met my cat, Brookline

Who is big, fierce, and white.

Brookline became boss

Because Blue wouldn't fight.

Blue went to puppy school,

He was the largest pup in his class.

Blue was a good student,

And learned commands fast.

Blue knows how to sit,
Lie down, come, and stay,
But his favorite thing to do
Is frolic and play.

Blue's favorite toy
Is a brown, soft, stuffed bear.
He chews it, shakes it, and
Tosses it in the air.

Blue likes when I take him
For hikes on wooded trails,
Where he smells yummy scents
And explores hills and dales.
But we have one problem
Because Blue's big and strong:
When I walk him in the neighborhood,
He pulls me along.

Blue often barks
And he sure likes to howl,
But I've never, ever
Heard him growl.

I thought Blue would make a good therapy dog,

Since he's kind to all he meets.

He had to pass a special test,

To prove he listens and is sweet.

It's official, Blue passed the test,

He travels from place to place.

He visits schools and nursing homes

To spread joy, humor, and grace.

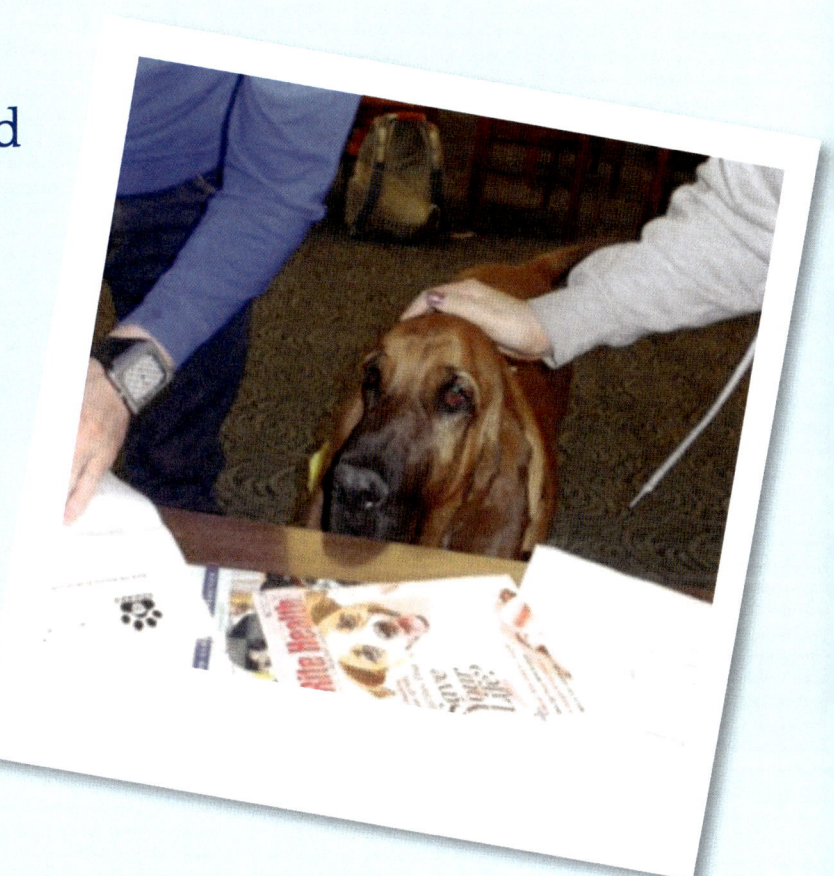

Blue visits lonely people,

Lets them pet his silky ears.

They smile and laugh when they see him,

He brightens their day with cheer.

Blue listens to children read their books,

They practice their words and sounds,

He pays special attention and is silent,

They like reading to a bloodhound.

Now when Jon visits Blue and I,

He's thrilled for Blue's success.

Jon hugs and praises Blue,

As he wears his therapy vest.

I am so very lucky

To have Blue hanging around.

And now he's your friend,

A large, red bloodhound.

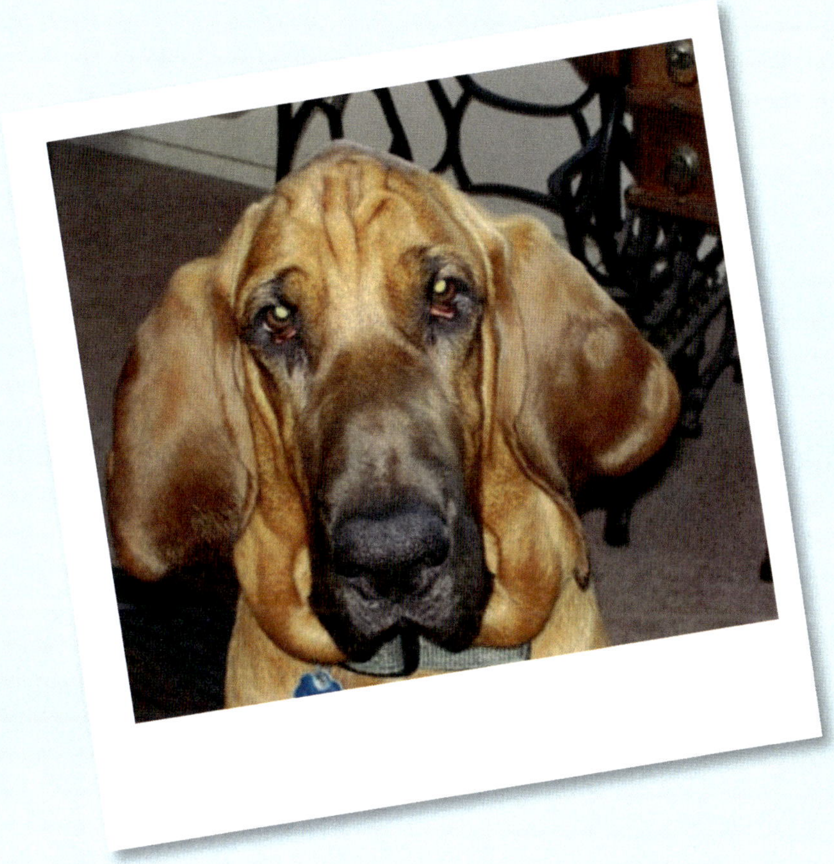

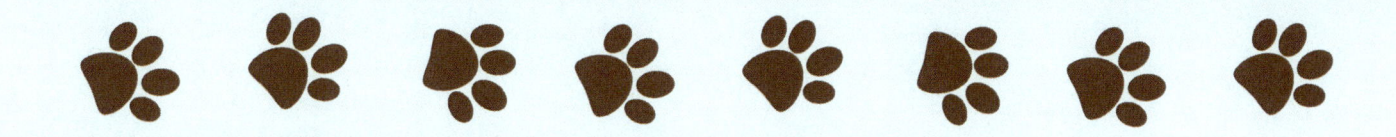

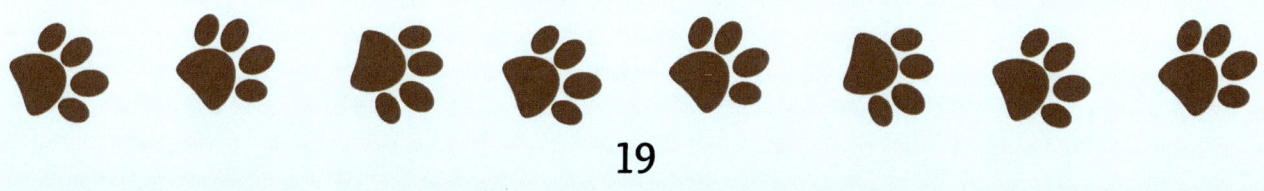

BLUE'S THERAPY BUDDIES

TAYLOR 		PUCK 		ELU

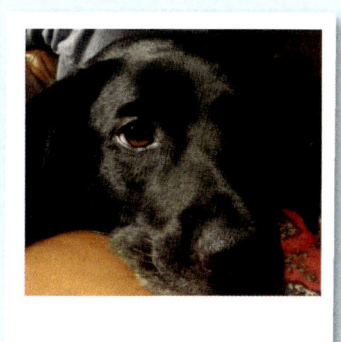

FLEURI   HAILEY   LASSIE   STAR

WHAT ARE THE CHARACTERISTICS OF A THERAPY DOG?

In order for dogs to be successful as therapy dogs, they must be friendly and obedient. The dogs must respond to the commands: sit, lie down, stay, come, and "leave it." The dogs must also not panic when they hear loud noises like fire drills. They are trained to be comfortable around wheelchairs, walkers, and canes.

WHO BENEFITS FROM VISITS WITH THERAPY DOGS?

- Seniors in long term care facilities
- Hospice patients, family members and staff
- Hospital patients
- Children struggling to read in schools and libraries
- At-risk teens
- Autistic children
- Patients during physical, occupational, speech, or cognitive therapy sessions
- Pets and their handlers

BLUE VISITS:

- Locust House, a senior housing apartment building
- Nursing homes: Carroll Lutheran Village and Golden Living Center
- A Juvenile Detention Center
- Eldersburg Elementary School
- West Middle School
- Libraries
- Hospice patients at Dove House
- Carroll Hospital Center
- State's Attorney's Office in Carroll County
- McDaniel College
- Fund raising events

Made in the USA
Middletown, DE
05 July 2020